American History:

The People & Events That Change American History

The Story of America

By John Stewart

All Rights Reserved. No part of this publication may be reproduced in any form or by any means, including scanning, photocopying, or otherwise without prior written permission of the copyright holder. Copyright © 2016

Disclaimer Notice:

Please note the information contained within this document is for educational purposes only. Every attempt has been made to provide accurate, up to date and reliable complete information no warranties of any kind are expressed or implied. Readers acknowledge that the author is not engaging in rendering legal, financial or professional advice.

By reading any document, the reader agrees that under no circumstances are we responsible for any losses, direct or indirect, which are incurred as a result of use of the information contained within this document, including – but not limited to errors, omissions, or inaccuracies.

Table of Contents

Chapter 1: Introduction
Chapter 2: Pennsylvania Anarchy
Chapter 3: The Revolutionaries
Chapter 4: The Anti-Federalists
Chapter 5: The Tariff of Abominations
Chapter 6: Slaves and Free Men
Chapter 7: A Nation by Compulsion
Chapter 8: The Panic Years
Chapter 9: The Federal Reserve Act
Chapter 10: 1929 and 1934
Chapter 11: American Internment Camps
Chapter 12: Kent State
Chapter 13: Occupy Wall Street and a Hopeful Conclusion
  Instant Access to Free Book Package!

Chapter 1: Introduction

Any attempt to describe any part of American history necessarily involves so much research that a person who takes the subject seriously soon finds themselves deluged by it all. Written records of the nation's early colonial days provide detailed information about what was happening in each colony. This occurred because each colony considered itself to be a new nation. Today, in the first half of the twenty-first century, we typically know very little about states other than ones in which we live because they are not important to us. We are all one unified country. The force of exoticism that drives people to delve into foreign languages and cultures often fails to drive them to delve into the histories of neighboring towns and states.

However, there is at least one aspect of American history that can be briefly described without the use of a great many words and which runs through the entirety of the nation's history. From the beginning of the very first colonies to the present day, there have always existed two groups of people: those who believed that a strong central government was necessary to safeguard the welfare of individual citizens and those who believed that a strong central government posed a danger to society in general.

Most of the struggles that have existed throughout American history have taken place between two groups with diametrically opposite ideas. These groups divided themselves into loyalists and revolutionaries; federalists and anti-federalists; slave owners and abolitionists; supporters of the war and conscientious objectors; suffragists who wished to vote and their opponents who did not wish them to vote; hippies and supporters of the Vietnam war; libertarians and the people who were in favor of the drug war; and finally anarchists who wanted to abolish the government and supporters of Donald Trump's presidential campaign who found themselves drawn to authoritarian ideas.

To describe each of these conflicts in turn would take up more space than I am willing to commit to any book of history. My purpose in writing this text is not to have it read by a handful of academics that delight in plodding through wordy manuscripts for the purpose of finding a quote to support their research. Rather, I write this book for the person working at a grocery store, the person driving a forklift at a warehouse, the person fixing roofs, cutting trees, and serving alcohol at local bars. I write this book for every person who cares to read it. Accordingly, I have kept it as short as I can with the understanding that each person's time is valuable.

If I have done my job with any competency at all, the overall theme should become clear from the most salient points I have chosen to dwell upon.

Chapter 2: Pennsylvania Anarchy

The historian Murray Rothbard discussed what happened in the Pennsylvania colony from 1681 to 1690 in his four-volume history called *Conceived in Liberty*. His findings suggest a state of affairs of an unprecedented nature existed in those days. Specifically, the state did not have a government. Though William Penn had been granted a land charter by Charles II in 1681, he had no way of enforcing the King's laws when the colony was first created. The colony was huge by the standards of those days. From Philadelphia to the modern town of West Alexander (a town located southwest of Pittsburgh along I-70) is 329 miles. From New Freedom in York County to Gillett in Bradford County is 198 miles. It can well be imagined that people limited to riding on horseback to travel anywhere might have had great difficulty in enforcing such laws as existed at the time. The colony was a vast tract of land that included not only the modern state of Pennsylvania itself, but also the state now known as Delaware.

The first constitution of the colony- then called frames of government or charters of privileges- did not exist until 1683. The charter was revised successively as the colonial government tried to figure out how to get people to obey its edicts. William Penn, himself a Quaker, imagined his colony as a "holy experiment." Penn received the land grant in exchange for an absolution of debt owed to Penn's father in the amount of 16,000 pounds.

Now, it must not be imagined that Pennsylvania was a colony inhabited only by Native Americans. Immigration from Europe was already underway. There were five hundred Swedish and Dutch residents already living on the western side of the Delaware River. They were informed of the new charter, which now bound them under William Penn's rule as governor of the colony. They were not asked to assent or dissent from the charter. It simply happened. As a result, what happened afterward becomes easy to understand.

In addition, after William Penn advertised his new colony to any who would listen as a bastion of religious tolerance where land could be had for cheap prices, people from all over Europe began flooding into the colony. Penn's purpose, besides providing a place where people all faiths could get along, was to extract taxes from the colonists in order to run the government. He would have to pay his tribute to the country who had granted him the colony provided that the king demanded such tribute in the first place.

The people that came to the new colony were composed of such a character as to make governance difficult, if not impossible. They were all self-selectors. They chose to be where they were. No one forced them go; no one had to. They set out to make something of themselves in a new land where they would have to start from scratch. They were pioneers and, as such, they had independent spirits. No one at that time would have uprooted his entire life, sailed across the Atlantic Ocean, and then braved harsh conditions in a strange place all for the purpose of placing himself under the rule of another man. Anyone who desired the security that came from the presence of a governmental authority did not need to move anywhere, for governments where everywhere present in Europe.

The people who settled in the colony did not want to pay taxes. Nor were they happy with the powers that the governor granted himself. Penn found himself in a quandary: it cost money to keep the government running, yet no one in the colony was willing to pay to keep the lights on. For all intents and purposes, the colonists wanted anarchy: that is, an absence of centralized authority.

His tax collectors and governmental agents were not particularly effective in collecting the money that Penn wished to be collected. Many of them were the same self-selectors who had chosen to move from Europe to the new continent. They yearned for freedom, just the same as everyone else. Moreover, many European countries had a history of demanding too much taxation from the people. Though the feudal system of lords and serfs was beginning to evaporate, it was nevertheless still imprinted upon the consciousness of European civilization. The great individualist writers and philosophers of the 18th and 19th centuries had not arrived yet. Étienne de La Boétie's work entitled *The Politics of Obedience: The Discourse of Voluntary Servitude* was the only philosophical work written to suggest that there might be something wrong with obeying governmental authority. Though it was written in the mid-16th century, the colonists of Pennsylvania appear to have been unaware of its existence. They arrived at their notions on their own, without assistance from anyone.

Had they not done so, the entire course of American history might have been different. Had the colonists all been happy taxpayers willing to go along with whatever William Penn wanted, the tradition of resisting taxation wherever and whenever it was put into place may not have begun. That tradition drove the American Revolution, the Whiskey Rebellion, and countless other landmark events in the nation's history. It all began in the quiet wilderness of Pennsylvania.

Chapter 3: The Revolutionaries

It is far more difficult to find a society in which local towns, cities, or states did not rebel against a centralized authority than those that did. Dissent, insurrection, rebellion, and civil war are the hazards that governments everywhere in the world must pay for continuing to stay in power. All sorts of people have all sorts of different opinions. When those opinions become strong enough, disagreements tend to occur. Since the nature of governmental authority is to discard and ignore any opinion that its agents do not hold themselves, nations large and small are never at peace with themselves, much less each other.

The year 69 AD is called the Year of the Four Emperors. It was a year in which four men claimed to be emperor of Rome. Only of them- Vespasian- managed to secure the position for himself. The other three emperors- Galba, Otho, and Vitellus- did not agree that Vespasian should be the emperor. They each had different ideas. As soon as the emperor's power became up for grabs, it soon transpired that various people were willing to enter into violent conflict to obtain such power.

This was not an isolated incident within Roman history. From the time of the Brothers Gracchi in the second century AD to the fall of the Roman Empire, civil strife was the norm rather than the exception. Civil wars abounded. Persecutions of minorities within the city and empire occurred on a regular basis. Millions of people died throughout Rome's history for the simple reason that people disagreed with one another.

The same pattern can be observed in any other nation. In Japan, the Battle of Sekigahara finalized the ascendancy of the Tokugawa Shogunate over the power of the Toyotomi clan. The Chinese civil war, which ended in 1949, saw the communist Mao Zedong defeat the nationalist Chiang Kai-shek. These are but two examples; there are many others. The nation of England, for example, has had so many violent usurpations of power throughout its history that it must be wondered why any king or queen sought the throne in the first place. Anywhere a history of government can be recorded will be found records of internecine struggles that stem from differences of opinion.

The normative behavior of people involved in these conflicts has always been that brothers and countrymen no longer hold allegiances to one another in the face of political upheaval. Neighbors will fight neighbors; fathers will fight sons. When once a situation that involves a national interest cannot be resolved peacefully, it will soon be resolved violently. Human nature, in which the ego of the individual tends to be held in greater esteem than the lives of others, suggests that people are difficult to control and near impossible to rule. This has not stopped governments of all sorts throughout history from trying to control and rule their subjects.

It did not stop the monarchy of King George III from trying to the rule the American colonists, all of whom had prospered from the increased autonomy that was afforded them by means of being so distantly removed from the English throne. In his book *Wealth of Nations,* Adam Smith describes colonial America as a vigorous place in which people worked hard to earn what they had. Years later, when Alexis de Tocqueville was sent to America from France for the ostensible purpose of studying America's prison system, he ended up writing a two-volume book called *Democracy in America.* Both Smith and de Tocqueville agreed on the same thing: America was a land of opportunity.

At least, that was the view that foreigners took from the outside. The reality of the American revolutionary spirit was quite different. Though there were people among the colonists who supported the notion of offering slaves a chance to earn their freedom, there was too much profit being made in the south for such an idea to be considered. The port town of Charlestown, South Carolina was, by the year 1770, making an enormous amount of money on the slave trade.

Slavery was, and always will be, a lucrative industry. Human slaves only cost the wages of the men assigned to kidnap them and the expenditures that arose from a journey across the ocean. Tribes in Africa could not resist European men with muskets and sabers. The slaves did not need to be kept in sanitary conditions, or fed well. It did not matter if they died on the way back. Property owners were willing to pay a high price for each individual slave, for a person working for free could produce unlimited value for any business venture. Slavery was just too profitable.

The result was that Lord Dunmore, a British governor, issued a proclamation saying that any slave who fought on the side of the British army would receive their freedom after the war was over. He kept his promise, though not before the African regiments of the time were subjected to racism and ill treatment. An impartial observer of the American Revolution would have seen the colonists promising freedom and not giving it while the British did not promise freedom and gave it anyway.

Because personal interest trumped morality, each colonist had to decide for themselves whether they wanted to support the revolution or support the King's government. Those who did support the king became known as loyalists. The colonists who supported a new form of government called the loyalists enemies of liberty (itself a phrase with some amount of hypocrisy in it). They were authoritarians who were afraid that chaos and anarchy would result if the king's government was overthrown. Some of them felt that freedom would come eventually, and that there was no need to use violence to secure it. Some of them believed that they had more to lose by severing ties with England, which would mean severing ties with the world's most powerful navy.

The loyalists were treated as enemies of the American people. They were tarred and feathered, and often ostracized out of their comfortable lifestyles. After the colonists proved victorious, thousands of them fled north to Canada. From the beginning, the fledgling nation adopted a "you're either with me or against me" stance. Many of the loyalists had done nothing more than express their support for the King. That was enough to earn them the derision and hatred of colonists trying to carve out a nation wherein they wouldn't have taxes imposed upon them.

It's worth mentioning that the vehemence that the colonists expressed against taxation was the same attitude that the Pennsylvania colonists had against William Penn imposing taxes upon them. Neither the residents of Penn's colony nor the revolutionaries wished to pay part of their earnings to a government that they felt did not represent them.

Less than ninety years passed before the colonists decided that they would not be able to resolve matters peacefully. In their view, they had to actively fight against the king's chosen representatives. Had the King of England responded to the petitions of the colonists, matters might have been different. However, that response would have posed a new problem: would the king then have to change his stated policy any time someone requested that he do so? That would be an impossible dilemma for any monarch who sought to be the absolute authority within all the territories that he ruled.

For any responsiveness to be had out of a governmental body, the system of governance itself had to be changed. It just so happened that the colonists who sought freedom from the English crown soon became worried that too much freedom might be a bad thing.

Chapter 4: The Anti-Federalists

A little less than five years after the signing of the Declaration of Independence, Maryland became the last state of the union to ratify the Articles of Confederation. Two years had passed after New Jersey ratified it in 1779. The American Revolution ended with the Treaty of Paris in September 1783. The colonists did not have an opportunity to observe the new American government under normal conditions for the first two years after the Articles became the law of the land. No one expected the government to run efficiently in wartime, not while battles could break out anywhere at any moment.

However, once the war ended, matters became quite different. The Articles of Confederation worked in such a way as to maintain as much of each state's sovereignty as possible. Each state had to send their own representatives to the nation's capital in order for the machinery of government to function. However, the nation's capital frequently changed from 1781 to 1789. Six different cities served as the national capital. The difficulty of finding one's way through the country, and the time it took to travel from Georgia to Philadelphia or from Maine to New York City made it difficult for representatives to participate in the government.

The result was that, as one year succeeded another, little to nothing was done in government while the Articles remained in effect. The veterans who participated in the war of independence had to be paid. The nation could not remain in debt forever. The government would have to resort to that most odious of practices: taxation.

Moreover, many colonists were apprehensive about having a nation that did not have a national defense. England was still a major power. France and Spain were not shy about investing time and effort into territory in North America. At the time, the fear was that any country with a half-decent military force would land wherever they pleased and roll up any city they wanted. Their victory over England had done nothing to convince them that they could rest easy. The English generals responsible for the war effort often did a slipshod job. No one expected that to always be the case.

Additionally, the new government was so weak that people began to fear that anarchy would result if the proper authority was not exerted. The desire for freedom that was felt so keenly under the rule of a foreign power had, within a few short years, become replaced by the desire to be, as George Washington put it, "an example to all nations."

Though just about everyone agreed that the government had to be amended, many people disagreed on what the rules of such a government would look like. The Constitutional Convention of 1787 met to hash out those rules. When it adjourned, it ended up with a document that it presented to the populace which, it was then supposed, would save the nation from the forces of chaos that waited to descend upon it at the first opportunity.

Though the convention had discharged its duty as best it could, presenting the document to the general public allowed anyone and everyone to weigh in on what they thought the constitution should look like. Some argued that there ought to be a bill of rights attached. Some argued that the document should be accepted exactly as it was. Still others thought that the constitution ought to be rejected.

They were dissenting voices in a country wherein the federalists- those who wished for a strong central government- influenced many of the media outlets so that only opinions in support of the constitution would appear in circulation. Furthermore, the newspapers that did exist only served their immediate areas. There was no such thing as a paper with a national readership.

To make matters worse, the federalist articles- many of which were written by Alexander Hamilton- were organized under a central theme and a single pseudonym. The anti-federalist articles were written by a variety of different people under all kinds of pen names. Among them were "Brutus," "Cato," and "Centinel." Each author had his own ideas and they often disagreed with one another.

The result was that, while the public debate raged over whether the Constitution ought to be accepted or not, the propaganda machine of the time largely worked in favor of the federalists. Popular anti-federalists Patrick Henry and George Mason found difficulty in stemming the tide of popular opinion. In many cases, the only ideas that people had been exposed to were those in favor of ratification.

The anti-federalists' suspicions that the office of president, then a novelty the world had never seen before, would soon turn into a monarchy proved to be correct. Nor did it take very long for the proof to arrive. During his first term as president, George Washington's government instituted a tax on whiskey that many people in the country found intolerable. Pennsylvanians in particular wanted nothing to do with it. Washington was forced to resort to the one solution that every executive authority in history has resorted to whenever organized disobedience arose: he sent in the troops.

The Whiskey Rebellion of 1791 proved that the federal government, acting as the ultimate arbiter of the law, would have the authority to levy taxes by means of violent coercion if such coercion was deemed necessary. Nor was that an isolated incident. Little pockets of resistance to federal edicts continued rising to the surface as a people accustomed to being free resisted attempts at being controlled.

Chapter 5: The Tariff of Abominations

The fundamental problem of all governmental spending is essentially this: people naturally try to safeguard what is theirs while they do not take as much care safeguarding what is not theirs. This is why governments large and small gravitate towards bankruptcy rather than a wise use of the resources they are given. Money that isn't earned by an individual is less important than money that came as a result of hard work.

Additionally, governments are forced to utilize the resources they have for the public good- or what may appear to be the public good. Any government that takes in taxes and refuses to spend it on either the military or on any public works project will soon be perceived as an organization to which no allegiance is owed. People like their governments in proportion to what they feel those governments will give them. A government that gives people nothing- or, even worse, gives them more trouble than they wish to endure- will find itself embattled to maintain its authority.

Such was the case when, under the presidency of John Quincy Adams, Congress passed the Tariff of Abominations. This became its colloquial nickname after it was passed. Political upheavals in Europe forced English merchants to sell their goods in America at a fraction of the price of what American merchants could sell them. In order to maintain American businesses, tariffs were placed on the importation of foreign goods. These tariffs were designed to keep the prices evenly matched.

The tariffs were favored by businessmen from New England, though not from businesses in the south. South Carolina took particular exception to the tariff of 1828. Resentment from the state built up so much that the state declared it unconstitutional. The tariff would not be enforced within the borders of the state.

Once more, the federal government found itself in the position of imposing its rules upon a group of people who disagreed with them.

However, the Nullification Crisis that arose in 1832 had its origins in more than just a disagreement between one particular state and the federal government. The issue derived from the notion of state's rights. A gradual erosion of state's rights had been ongoing since the Constitution's inception. In 1798, the state of Virginia adopted a resolution in response to the Aliens and Sedition Act, passed into law that same year. The resolution was written by James Madison and Thomas Jefferson. A similar resolution had been adopted in Kentucky.

One paragraph of the resolution reads as follows:

> That this state having by its Convention, which ratified the federal Constitution, expressly declared, that among other essential rights, "the Liberty of Conscience and of the Press cannot be cancelled, abridged, restrained, or modified by any authority of the United States," and from its extreme anxiety to guard these rights from every possible attack of sophistry or ambition, having with other states, recommended an amendment for that purpose, which amendment was, in due time, annexed to the Constitution; it would mark a reproachable inconsistency, and criminal degeneracy, if an indifference were now shewn, to the most palpable violation of one of the Rights, thus declared and secured; and to the establishment of a precedent which may be fatal to the other.

The resolution's argument was that, since the state of Virginia had approved of the Constitution, they could at a later date express their disapproval by anything they felt to be unconstitutional- i.e., "the most palpable violation of one of the Rights." The fear was that once the Constitution was approved, the federal government would make whatever laws it wanted without consulting the states. It had no legal obligation to do so. All it required for a law to be passed was the approval of Congress and the signature of the president. The government could then enforce the law throughout the entire nation if it so chose. This would leave the states with only two choices: compliance or disobedience.

South Carolina chose disobedience. Andrew Jackson sent a Force Bill to Congress. This bill asked Congress for the use of force against South Carolina. Jackson wanted to take American troops and march on the state for disobeying a federal edict. This was in response to South Carolina's Nullification Convention, which declared the tariffs illegal and unenforceable inside the state. Both Governor James Hamilton and Governor Robert Hayne were of a single mind on this point: the federal government could not enforce a law that was forbidden by the Constitution.

Jackson's response eclipsed the original issue. Suddenly, it was no longer about whether the state should have to pay the tariff. It was about whether the federal government would use a violent military to ensure that its will be done. Governor Hayne created a militia of 27,000 who were pledged to defend Charleston if a military conflict came. South Carolina was ready to go to war for a principle in which it strongly believed.

Andrew Jackson did all he could to inflame the issue. He found the notion of nullification to be absurd. The union could not survive as long as states could pick and choose which laws they wanted to follow and which they did not. He was doing exactly what James Madison feared a representative of the federal government might do. He was imposing his will on anyone who disagreed with him.

In 1830, when asked if he had any messages to pass along to the people of the state, he replied:

Yes I have; please give my compliments to my friends in your State and say to them, that if a single drop of blood shall be shed there in opposition to the laws of the United States, I will hang the first man I can lay my hand on engaged in such treasonable conduct, upon the first tree I can reach.

Fortunately, it did not come to bloodshed. A compromise was reached. The tariff was lightened. Each party got what they wanted. Washington, D.C. got a resolution to a vexing problem. South Carolina was able to prove that they could change a federal law if they chose to do so.

There was only one problem: neither side quite forgot the animosity that it bore towards the other.

Chapter 6: Slaves and Free Men

The abolitionist movement in America was already beginning to take shape when the Constitution was written. Nowhere in the document would anyone dare refer to a slave as a slave. For the purpose of counting a state's population and determining how many elected officials would serve in the government, a slave was three-fifths of a person. He could not vote. He could not run for office. A slave had no say in the laws which governed him. For a nation which had strove with great difficulty to ensure freedom for themselves and their posterity, the question of whether some men should enjoy that freedom while others did not became a central theme of the 19th century.

The northern states of the union took the lead in dealing with slavery. Vermont abolished it 1777. Pennsylvania's constitution of 1780 abolished it as well. The constitution of Massachusetts declared all men to be equal. The schism that would later develop between north and south was centered on a single issue: whether all men would be free regardless of skin color or whether some men should be free while others were not. The issue was primarily driven by self-interest. Transitioning away from a slave-labor economy would prove difficult for the south. The leaders there saw that it was cheaper to pay their labor force nothing.

The passage of time only exacerbated the underlying issues. France abolished slavery in 1794. The international slave trade was prohibited by the United Kingdom and the United States in 1807. The Slavery Abolition Act of 1833 abolished slavery in the United Kingdom. Slavery had been decreasing in Canada until it was made illegal in 1834. Meanwhile, the slaves who lived in the south and who were born in the south had no way to escape from the conditions imposed upon them. The citizens of the northern states, who had lived for decades without slavery, began to question why other states were still doing it.

This is not to say that manumissions did not exist at all. A slave was considered the property of his or her owner. The owner could dispose of the slave in whatever way he saw fit. Those who believed that slavery was wrong could choose to free their slaves. The slaves who were freed had no other choice but to move north in order to avoid being captured a second time. Almost no slave that had been kidnapped from Africa had any hope of returning there, much less of reconnecting with the people with whom they had lived.

During the first half of the 19th century, there were many parts of America which had not been recognized as official states. Missouri was one of those territories. The Tallmadge Act of 1819 sought to abolish the practice of slavery in Missouri. The Act was proposed by James Tallmadge Jr., a citizen of New York.

The issue at hand was this: the population of the north had grown. The slave population of the south had grown as well. But slaves were only counted as ⅗ of a person by the census. As a result, the southern states that had not abolished slavery sent fewer representatives to Congress. Some slave owners feared that politicians from the north would hold a majority in Congress regardless of which party was voted for, or who was elected. The only way they could solve this problem was to abolish slavery. This was a prospect that they relished even less than losing their influence in the government. They would either voluntarily give up the right to conduct business as they saw fit, or they would be compelled to free all their slaves at once by means of a federal law.

The Missouri Compromise of 1820 did nothing to keep southern slave owners from thinking that they would be dictated to. They feared that they would be told what they could and could not do. Such was their preference for slave-trading that they continued bringing slaves into the country in violation of the 1807 prohibition. The government in Washington found that it could not control the action of individuals who did not wish to be controlled. That slavery is an immoral, reprehensible practice meant very little to the people who owned slaves. They wanted autonomy, even while they refused to grant their fellow man the very thing they cherished so much.

Ironically, one of the groups that arose out of a desire to see slavery maintained in America was the American Colonization Society. The Society was formed in 1816 by Robert Finley. It was composed mostly of southern slave owners who were tired of having their slaves seeing the example of free black people in the north. They proposed to return those people back to Africa. The thought was that the slaves would eventually lose the notion that they should be free because other people like themselves should be free.

Abolitionists- many of which were Quakers- supported the Society based on the notion of repatriating black citizens to the continent of their birth. The Society proved to be one of the very few groups that sought to do something about black people in which both those who supported and those who opposed slavery were able to find common ground.

In 1821, the Society helped found the colony of Liberia. Liberia was intended as a place for free black Americans to go. As racism was rampant at that time, and equality did not truly exist, thousands of African Americans were willing to give the colony a try. The colony prospered so much that it was declared an independent state in 1847. By the year 1867, the Society had sent over thirteen thousand people to Liberia. The thirteenth amendment to the Constitution made the Society unnecessary; as such, it stopped repatriating black people to Africa.

The men and women who were quick enough to leave America before the Civil War had lucky stars. Those who remained were not so lucky. The Fugitive Slave Act of 1793 mandated that any slave who escaped from his master should be returned to that master. This Act was used to justify manhunts, and any number of other atrocities. The Act paved the way for public lynching in the south that were often performed with the assistance of local law enforcement. If a slave could not make himself free simply by escaping his captivity, then he would always the property of his master. Anything might be done to him- and anything was.

The northern states that opposed slavery ignored the law. They let escaped slaves remain. This helped facilitate the existence of the Underground Railroad. The organization began in the early 19th century. It reached its height in the middle of the century. The number of people who escaped slavery is difficult to pin down. The census has the figure around 6,000. Some reports claim as many as 30,000 fled. Over 5,000 court cases were recorded for runaway slaves. Harriet Tubman was once quoted as saying, "I freed a thousand slaves. I could have freed a thousand more if they knew they were slaves."

The Underground Railroad had a profound effect upon slave owners all across the south. The work of the American Colonization Society was being undone. Slaves had to be guarded and watched, lest they run away. Many of them had no desire to do so; they saw themselves in a hopeless situation from which no escape was possible. It was as if all the appliances in a modern house had grown legs. What had been counted on before as a matter of routine became an uncertainty. An inclination not to enforce the Fugitive Slave Act rankled in the south. They believed that the law had been put there for a reason. It had to be observed.

No historical person from that time ever made a recorded observation that South Carolina wished not to observe the tariff of 1828 while insisting that the Fugitive Slave Act be enforced. The law was nothing more than a tool that people used to gain an advantage over others. Ethics and morality rarely entered into it.

Chapter 7: A Nation by Compulsion

Anyone who visits Fort Sumter in South Carolina will be immediately struck by how small it is. It looks like it could house perhaps twenty people and two cannons. It is essentially a small pit around which fortifications were placed. No one who goes there today would believe that such a small, unassuming place could serve as the catalyst for one of the world's most significant events.

The events that led up to Fort Sumter were, by 1860, becoming more apparent every year. Former Whig-turned-Republican Abraham Lincoln was considered by many in South Carolina to be the worst president for the interests of the state. Politicians of those days believed that an abolition of slavery would lead to the collapse of the state's economy. They promised that if a Republican was elected in 1860, they would secede from the Union.

This promise was made real by a meeting of the South Carolina General Assembly in November of that year. The Assembly passed a motion declaring Lincoln's election to be a "Hostile Act." The question of whether a state would have any say in what happened at the federal level came up once more. South Carolina's position was that the majority should not always rule. If every state but one votes for the president of their choice, that one state considers itself to receive a bad result. The desire for autonomy remained strong with the citizens of the state. This had not changed in the seventy-three years since the Constitution was ratified.

Anti-federalist sentiment had been building for decades. The situation had reached such a point that, in his correspondence to nine men from Virginia, Congressmen John McQueen wrote:

In the great and momentous movement which our people have been able to make with unprecedented unanimity, after years of insult, robbery and patience, we have not been unmindful of the character and interests of your noble Old Dominion, whose warriors, statesmen and patriots have cast a lustre over her sisters identical in interest with her, and, in my judgment, soon to be identified with us in a common destiny, absolved from all ties with enemies who, in violation of every obligation which should have been sacred to the memory of a common ancestry, would murder our citizens, burn our houses, and poison even our women and children.

It is a source of unfeigned joy to me to believe, as I do, that "Virginia yet in time will surely stand like South Carolina, a free, sovereign and independent State, ready to unite with her Southern sisters."

This passage serves to demonstrate that the formation of a Southern confederation had already been in contemplation for some time. The audacious nature of the letter in which McQueen suggests that the state of Virginia will soon be ready to join such a confederation demonstrates the echoes of the Virginia Resolution of 1798. The same atmosphere which made the Resolution possible also, in later years, made it possible for open rebellion against the Union. Any rebellion that takes place must be grounded in the rights of the individual- even if the people who espouse those rights don't really believe in them. If no one believes they ought to do something, they won't do it. Belief always comes before action.

Had not the people of South Carolina believed that they should be able to determine whether they should obey any set of laws or not, Fort Sumter would never have happened. It's doubtful whether the Civil War would have taken place without the tariff of 1832, or without the debates that sprang up regarding whether the Constitution should be ratified. Anyone who does not understand why tyrannical societies engage in heavy censorship of everything with which it disagrees need only understand this: irreconcilable ideological differences tore an entire nation apart. The American Civil War wasn't the first time this happened in the history of world. Given the state of the present world suggests that it won't be the last time either.

The first shots of the war were fired by recruits from the Citadel attempting to prevent a ship named *Star of the West* from resupplying and reinforcing the base. At this time, Fort Sumter was being occupied by Union Army troops. Though such distinctions as Union and Confederate had not existed yet, the result was much the same. Neither President James Buchanan nor President Abraham Lincoln was willing to abandon the fort. Within the first few months of his presidency, Lincoln was determined to take a stand on this issue. He did not want to back down on any account.

The South Carolina state government discovered that it could starve the base out. By April 1861, the base's supplies would be exhausted. The troops would be forced to retreat or starve to death. When April did come around, the Confederacy had been established. It was formed in February of 1861; a month later, its Constitution was put into effect. Its capital was in Montgomery, Alabama. Its first president was Jefferson Davis, who was elected by popular acclaim. Regardless of how the situation in Fort Sumter was going to be resolved, the citizens of the American south had just had enough.

The Union army troops evacuated Fort Sumter on April 13, 1861 after intense fighting. Battles for control of the Fort took place in April and September of 1863. The Confederate forces repelled the Union troops. It was until February of 1865 that the Confederate troops finally withdrew from the fort. The American Civil War ended in May of that year with a Union victory.

President Lincoln had been assassinated in April 1865 four days after Robert E. Lee wrote a letter of surrender to Jefferson Davis. Davis dissolved the Confederate government on May 5th. Afterward, Davis was imprisoned for two years until he moved to Quebec to join his family. In 1868, he received a presidential pardon from Andrew Johnson. In 1875, he turned down an election to Congress in order to serve as Texas A&M's first president. The university was then called the Agricultural and Mechanical College of Texas.

Some effects of the war were felt immediately while others took longer to be observed. The South's economy was devastated during the war. Entire cities were burned to the ground. Though the Reconstruction Era lead to the Industrial Revolution, no one living at the time had any sense that that would happen. Some people found themselves living in grinding poverty. The slaves that were freed still dealt with racism that prevented them from being upwardly mobile. African Americans still had to move north if they wanted good opportunities. Running for office and voting was still out of the question. Frederick Douglass running as Victoria Woodhull's Vice President with the Equal Rights Party was an exception, not the rule.

After the Civil War, talk of secession never got any further than talk. No one ever put it into action. In the 21st century, secession movements have cropped up all across the country. States such as California, Texas, and New Hampshire have people within them who wish to divest themselves from the federal government. However, the boldness that once appeared among the people of South Carolina is not present. America is not perceived as fifty separate nations joined together for common cause. It is viewed as a nation with fifty provinces. The Civil War served to bind the country together in a way that nothing else could.

That binding, once perceived to be a positive, is now turning into a negative, deleterious force. Requiring the country's fifty states to remain in the nation, by force if necessary, leaves no possibility of the states to correct the bad behavior on the part of the federal government. Though each state has its own laws and its own particular sub-cultures, every region of the country can be victimized by aggressive federal agents pursuing their own agendas. Once it became established that violence was an effective way of securing one particular objective or other, governments all around the world have increasingly resorted to the use of force to resolve its problems.

As long as people were incapable of resisting, there was no reason for authority figures to rein themselves in. They could do whatever they wanted. Every protracted encounter between the citizens of America and the government of America demonstrates this principle. Nations had always fought other nations;

governments had always oppressed its own people on account of religion; after the Civil War, governments began oppressing people for disobedience to its dictates.

The irony of Abraham Lincoln's legacy is not that he freed black slaves in the south, but that he bound an entire nation of people and their progeny in servitude to a central authority with whom they may or may not have wished to serve. The result was the same as when Soviet Russia conquered various western European nations at the end of World War II, when Nazi Germany conquered Poland, when the British Empire conquered India, or when any other invading force conquered a group of indigenous people. The choice of whether to join or stay was taken away from the individual citizen from the states. In turn, this left the individual little choice but to leave the country or remain trapped inside a nation that may or may not represent his interests.

The Civil War turned America from a nation of cooperation into a nation of compulsion.

Chapter 8: The Panic Years

In retrospect, economic panics appear to be a normal function of America's economy. Leading up to the establishment of the Federal Reserve System in 1913, there were five separate periods of panic: 1873, 1884, 1893, 1901, and 1907. This chapter will briefly describe each panic in turn so that the subsequent events of 1913 may be fully comprehended.

The Panic of 1873 resulted from several factors coming together all at once. The US dollars inflated after the Civil War. Investment in railroads was at an all-time high. Many of those investments failed with the result that the money spent on them ended up being wasted. A great deal of that money came from the federal government in its attempts to reconstruct the economy it had destroyed. The Franco-Prussian War that raged from 1870 to 1871 decimated Europe's economy. Two city-wide fires worsened the situation: Chicago in 1871 and New York in 1872. All of these factors put together led to a run on the nation's various banks.

The Coinage Act of 1873 de-monetized silver. This began what is called "the gold standard." People who privately owned silver bullion had the right to have their silver pressed into official government currency. The Act was created after it was feared that discoveries of silver mines would cause silver to drastically inflate, thus causing the price of gold to drop as well. The result was that while people could trade silver for money, people could not turn their silver into money. This led to the issuance of silver certificates in 1878.

When the panic manifested itself in 1873, people found that they had fewer coins to rely upon. The two-cent piece, the three-cent piece and a coin called the half dime were discontinued. The uncertainty that resulted caused a loss of confidence in the government's management of the economy.

President Ulysses Grant had decided to retract the government's money supply during a period when investment capital was greatly desired to fund railroad projects across the nation. The companies that funded the railroads- Jay Cooke & Company in particular- found themselves unable to keep doing so. The Northern Pacific Railroad depended on loans from private companies to continue operating. Private companies relied on loans from the government to keep operating. When the government decided to stop giving out loans, the private companies no longer had money to give, which meant that railroads no longer could afford to fund their operations.

The plan to reconstruct the American economy had encountered a significant difficulty. The Panic of 1873 led to a depression that lasted until 1879. The depression left a deep impression upon the people of the country. Suddenly, nothing was for sure anymore.

Three years passed before the economy entered a recession that lasted until 1885. Another panic sprang up in 1884. In comparison to the events of 1873, the panic of 1884 was short-lived. It was caused by the banks lending out money that it could not earn back. Thousands of investment firms failed. Among them were Grant & Ward, the Marine Bank of New York, and the Penn Bank of Pittsburgh. Confidence of Wall Street practices dropped even further than it had been. When the New York Clearing House bailed out banks who were at risk of failure, the public was not reassured.

The Panic of 1893 came shortly after the President Grover Cleveland took office. European investors began a run on gold held by the US Treasury. To them, having gold was preferable to having paper money. With two economic panics behind them, citizens of the United States began withdrawing money from their banks. They had gone through it all twice before; a depression and recession both within twenty years had not been forgotten. With no choice but to stop giving out money, Cleveland's government created a credit crunch. There was less investment capital to be had. A panic that occurred in England at the same time caused European investors to sell off all their American stocks; this caused publicly-traded companies to lose money as their stocks fell.

Company after company failed as the dominos fell. Unemployment rose to nineteen percent. Homeowners could no longer afford their mortgages; they left behind homes they had just built. Uncertainty in Wall Street turned into distrust. The ideas of Karl Marx and Friedrich Engels took hold as people grasped for any explanation as to why things had gone so badly and so often. From the perspective of the middle-class American worker, a bunch of rich people in fancy suits were screwing up the economy. The notion of income inequality had never existed in America before; rich people were rich, poor people were poor, and anyone who made money for themselves were to be congratulated. Things changed when personal opportunity was prevented and stifled by strangers in a distant city.

The recession that followed lasted until 1898, by which time the economy was ready to fall apart again.

The Panic of 1901 was caused by the first crash of the New York Stock Exchange. The crash was caused by a few large companies trying to buy up as much stock of Northern Pacific Railway as they could.

The Northern Securities Company was formed after the crisis. The Company controlled so much of the country's railroads that President Roosevelt's Justice Department sued the company under the Sherman Antitrust Act of 1890. In 1904, the Supreme Court ruled five to four against the Company. The railroad companies that had been consolidated under the Company were forced to operate independently once more.

The Panic of 1907 occurred during a time of economic recession. A group of investors tried to corner the market on the United Copper Company. The scheme failed. Afterward, regional banks across the nation withdrew as much of their money as they could from the banks in New York. The Stock Exchange plummeted. If not for J.P. Morgan, John Rockefeller, and the US Treasury bailing out banks on the verge of collapse, the situation may have become much worse than what it was.

However, after five panics, one crash, one near-crash, and persistent instability, the government decided that the banks had to be regulated. This would lead to one of the worst governmental actions in American history.

Chapter 9: The Federal Reserve Act

The Aldrich-Vreeland Act of 1908, proposed by Senator Nelson Aldrich of Rhode Island, established the National Monetary Commission. The purpose of the commission was to study the banking laws of America in comparison with those of Europe. The prevailing belief of the time was that American law were not sufficient to prevent big banks from crashing the economy at will, if they chose to do so. The richest bankers in the country were viewed in a negative light. The farmers and factory workers of America could not protect themselves except by keeping their money out of the banks. Even that might not be enough. Whether they were employed or unemployed was completely out of their hands. Something had to be done.

The Commission generated thirty reports from 1909 to 1912. The reports detailed economic conditions and banking law of as many other western countries as could possibly be found. However, for all the information that was accumulated, the public was largely left in the dark about what the commission had found, and what it recommended. The Commission proposed that America reinstate a central bank. The last such institution had been the Second Bank of the United States. It had existed until 1836 when, after failing to secure a renewal for its charter as a governmental agency, it became a private company. The bank subsequently went out of business in 1841.

When he ran for election in 1911, Democrat Woodrow Wilson opposed any plan involving a central bank. However, in 1913, when the Federal Reserve was passed by in the House of Representatives and in the Senate, Wilson took only five days to sign it. The Act became law on the day after Christmas- December 26, 1913.

A printed collection of Wilson's speeches reveals a man who disliked the way society was progressing. He did not approve of the introduction of the corporation.

He did not like that people had to work dangerous machines that they had no hand in repairing. He did not like that people worked for companies who, in his words, often went against the public good. Though he does not talk of wealth redistribution, many of Wilson's speeches reveal a socialist vein of thought. He was a man who grew up during the various panics, depressions, and recessions. The inability of rich men to act in favor of what benefited the public left a deep impression on him. He did not, as some have suggested, bitterly regret having created the Federal Reserve. He had seen what had happened when banks were left alone to do what they wanted. He sought to intervene in a progressive manner. He would do what he thought was right for the country as a whole, even if no one else would.

The Federal Reserve was an organization that was like nothing America had ever seen. In addition to the bank in Washington, D.C., twelve regional banks were incorporated. The Federal Reserve System was overseen by a group of seven governors. Though it had been created by an act of Congress, it was not part of the United States Treasury. The Federal Reserve was endowed with the power to print money- now called Reserve Notes- whenever the governors deemed it necessary.

The initial twenty-year charter for the Reserve system was renewed in 1933 during the Great Depression. Since then, very few politicians have come forward to question the organization's existence until the present day when Republican Ron Paul, running for president in 2008 and 2012, made one of his platforms an audit and abolition of the Fed. Public opinion on the Federal Reserve remains divided: some believe that it is a force for public good. Others believe that it is an organization that creates more harm than good.

The evidence since the Fed's inception in 1914 suggests that the second conclusion is the correct one. From 1914 to 2016- the year in which this book was written- the US dollar has inflated by 2271.1%. Inflation of the printed dollar is caused by more dollars being put into circulation via the printing press. Under ordinary conditions, the government would have an incentive to limit the money supply, rather than expand it. This would keep the dollar strong in relation to other international currencies.

However, the monetary situation of the entire 20th century and the beginning of the 21st century has been anything other than normal. A series of endless wars combined with an increase welfare benefits and recipients to cause the federal government to spend more money than it earned. The Federal Reserve was, and continues to be, forced to print more money every year in order to pay off the interest on the loans that the government takes out from other countries.

This begins a self-destructive pattern that eventually will resolve in a financial collapse. The more money that the Federal Reserve prints, the more the value of the dollar inflates. When the dollar inflates, it becomes worth less than it was before. When it becomes worth less than it was before, it is able to buy less today than it did yesterday. Though the specific amount of each loan remains the same, the government isn't able to spend as much as it once did.

This principle can be demonstrated in a simple manner. One day, a cantaloupe, a book, and a bottle of wine cost twenty dollars. Another day, sometime later, twenty dollars can buy a book and a bottle of wine, but not a cantaloupe. American consumers all across the country have experienced this dilemma within the last fifty years.

Because the dollar doesn't buy as much as it used to, the price of goods and services rise all across the supply chain. The business owner who wants to stock a bottle of wine, a book, and a cantaloupe in his store sooner prefers to raise his prices so that he can get more money to keep buying what he wants. If he did not do this, he would one day find his store half-empty.

Likewise, if the government spent money within its budget, it would be forced to reduce its current expenditures. Thus far, the government has chosen to keep spending and keep borrowing rather than making tough choices about what it should and should not fund. The Federal Reserve serves as an enabler to the federal government's irresponsible spending.

It appears highly unlikely that anyone in 1913 saw that such a circumstance would unfold. They were thinking of preventing economic instability. They were thinking of the good of the country. They were hoping that they could stop the panics from happenings. Their hopes were greatly dashed.

Chapter 10: 1929 and 1934

The reparations that the Allied powers demanded of Germany after World War I left the Weimar Republic bankrupt. Its currency was so worthless that people used banknotes to start fires in fireplaces. In spite of such an example, and in spite of evidence to the contrary, the people of America had more faith in their economy than they ever had before. Wilson's economy during the war was a managed socialist economy. The socialists in charge of the economy, such as Eugene Debs, despaired when the armistice was declared. They wanted the managed economy to continue. It did not.

Glutted by their success in the war and optimistic about the future, no one believed that another panic would come again. Fewer people thought that the crash to end all crashes would come. Optimism led to speculation, investment, and easy credit. People spent, and continued spending. Consumers were building up debts while sales decreased. Each person only had so much money to spend before they had to stop spending. When sales decreased, company profits decreased.

An economist named Roger Babson warned in September of 1929 that a crash was coming. The London Stock Market crashed on September 20th. Leading up to Black Tuesday, the American market was unstable. The historical records from the time suggest that the events of Thursday, October the twenty-fourth were taken completely by surprise. The Stock Market continued to struggle through Friday and Monday until Tuesday came around. The Market lost thirty billion dollars between October 28th and October 29th.

Though Black Tuesday heralded the beginning of the Great Depression, it was not a cause in and of itself. It was simply an indication of what was already happening. Too much confidence had been placed in the market. No one thought that what happened in the Weimar Republic could happen in America. People with money to spend invested it incautiously.

Unemployment, starvation, homelessness, and despair followed. President Franklin Roosevelt promised and delivered a series of laws aimed at protecting the American consumer. That was what he told the public, at least.

The Gold Reserve Act of 1934 proved to be something completely different. Up until that time, the American people traded in paper money and gold. When Roosevelt signed the Act into law, private ownership of gold was expressly forbidden. Trading gold for goods and services was illegal. Any gold that was owned privately had to be turned into the US Treasury in exchange for paper money. Anyone who understood inflation at that time would have seen the bad deal they were getting. The price of gold compared with the price of the US dollar would only rise with time as money continued being printed- especially during wartime.

The government followed through with its prohibition on the private ownership of gold. Four cases, collectively known as the Gold Clause Cases, were brought before the Supreme Court in which the court was asked to decide whether the government could legally punish people for owning and trading gold. The Supreme Court decided in favor of the government. Additionally, foreign companies with gold in the United States had their gold seized.

The Act, and Roosevelt's Executive Order 6102, was aimed not at protecting the economy as the government claimed, but rather at nothing more than a confiscation of wealth. The government declared that a person's private property was no longer their property. After silver and gold had been declared illegitimate currencies, there was nothing left but paper money. It was the one currency that had been distrusted and suspected of being valueless by people who were accustomed to using rare metals to conduct their business.

Chapter 11: American Internment Camps

Once America had become a nation where the individual states could not secede without risking a military action, the population of each state was at the mercy at the government. Binding all the states together in a single union created a hegemony in which national policy was always implemented upon each state, sometimes after a period of resistance that rarely- if ever- served to nullify any policy. Though America's slaves had been freed after the Civil War, much work remained to be done before every person was treated equally.

The federal government's policies with regards to race tended towards inequality during the beginning of the 20th century. The 1896 case of *Plessy v. Ferguson* confirmed each states to practice discrimination. In 1913, Woodrow Wilson separated white troops and black troops from each other in the military. Jim Crow laws cropped up all over the south. The federal government did little to check those laws until the 1954 case of *Brown v. Board of Education.* With legal sanction to do whatever they chose, racial tensions got worse and worse with the passage of each year.

My analysis of this period in history does not suggest that people are always racist, or that persecution will always exist as long as the human race exists. Such a supposition presupposes that human beings have an innate tendency to treat each other badly. The evidence that does exist- extraordinarily expensive though it is- suggests that people are good when they are out of power and bad when they are in power. The majority of evil that is done in this world is, and always been, derived from people who abuse their authority. The person who doesn't abuse their authority is far rarer than the person who does.

The Civil Rights issues of the twentieth century demonstrate this pattern. Police officer and sheriff assisted in the lynching of black men. The Tulsa Riots in 1921 took place because the law enforcement of the time did not make a point of checking the racism that was taking place. Rather, the laws that did exist tended towards mistreatment and inequality.

In such an atmosphere, internment camps arose. In Germany, concentration camps for Jewish people and political dissenters were constructed. In America, camps for Japanese-American citizens were constructed based on the suspicion that any person of Japanese descent living in America might be a spy. Hundreds of thousands of people were rounded up and imprisoned.

No organization, large or small, has ever perpetrated crimes on the magnitude of those committed by the federal government. Arresting people without trial and holding them against their will can be called nothing else except a crime. The people arrested weren't allowed to face their accusers. They weren't allowed to defend themselves in court. They weren't allowed to appeal their sentences.

When such an action is committed by a private citizen, it is called kidnapping. The charge that is levied in court is called false imprisonment. The Japanese-Americans who were sent to internment camps as a result of Executive Order 9066 in 1942 were falsely imprisoned. In 1944, the Supreme Court heard a case brought by Fred Korematsu, a Japanese-American citizen who was brought to court for evading internment.

People like Korematsu had no recourse other than actively disobeying or resisting the government. Rather than serving to protect the freedoms of individual people, the law instead served to deprive individual freedom. Rather than creating a country in which people could be treated equally, the law served to create even more inequality than that which had existed naturally. Rather than solving problems, the law served to create problems. President Roosevelt's internment camps demonstrate this principle as had many other laws that passed the government at all levels of operation.

More than seventy years after the end of World War II, no tangible evidence has been found to suggest that a spy network of any kind existed among the Japanese-American citizens who were detained by the government. The war effort was not influenced by the detainees giving actionable intelligence on what the Japanese military was planning.

The personal cost to the detainees was severe. Many people lost personal property. They were taken away from jobs they had been accustomed to doing. They had to start over from scratch. Congress took three years to pass any law that would compensate detainees for their loss of property and income. It was called the American Japanese Claims Act. It turned out that since the IRS had destroyed their tax records from the period of 1939 to 1942. Additionally, in the face of being dislocated, many people had difficulty preserving their financial records. In the end, 37 million dollars was distributed out of 148 million dollars that was requested.

In took another twenty-eight years until President Gerald Ford, in 1976, declared the internment of Japanese-American citizens a mistake that would not be repeated. However, for all his good intentions, Ford could only speak for himself. He could not anticipate what would happen when people suspected of being terrorists would be sent to a prison camp in Guantanamo Bay, Cuba.

The same pattern emerged: just after an unprovoked attack, people of a certain ethnicity, in this case Muslims, were detained against their will. They were not given a trial. They were not allowed to face their accusers. Their entire lives were disrupted at the say-so of one particular authority or another. In spite of all the work that was done in name of doing away with racism, it sprang up with alarming ferocity.

Nor does their strange fear of a certain ethnic group called Islamophobia doesn't appear to be going away anytime soon. This fear appears to be driving today's leaders towards unproductive courses that they would not otherwise pursue. These leaders are driven by intense fear and paranoia much as the leaders during World War II were driven by suspicion of anyone who might be colluding with the enemy of those days.

In the face of national patriotism and all the evils that come with it, individual rights tend to be forgotten. This is the single principle that has inspired the book you are now reading. If it anything I have written thus far is true, then it is the duty of the people who understand these things to inform those who do not, for it cannot be doubted that no minority is safe as long as a centralized authority exists.

The smallest minority is a minority of one. Each person is different from one another. No two people are alike. Therefore, the more power any leader gets, the more at risk the individual becomes. The world of the last hundred years is full of examples of how people in power committed genocide, ethnic cleansing, and various Great Leaps Forward in the name of ideological purity. The result was death and destruction on a massive scale. Every leader Josef Stalin to Mao Zedung to Pol Pot to Adolf Hitler to George W. Bush has demonstrated that the life, liberty, and property of the individual will be neither respected nor protected.

This pattern of behavior can be further demonstrated by events that occurred in a certain university in Ohio in the year 1970.

Chapter 12: Kent State

Following the death of President John F. Kennedy in 1963, the American public had become increasingly skeptical of the government. The Vietnam War had become a poorly managed boondoggle whose original purpose- stopping the spread of communism- was dubious at best. The General Secretary of the Communist Party Nikita Khrushchev had wanted to rule by popular acclaim, rather than by fear and murder as Josef Stalin had. When Leonid Brezhnev took over the position in 1964, he announced a series of reforms intended to boost the Soviet economy. At the time, there was every indication that tensions between both countries would wear themselves out. The Cold War was beginning to thaw.

The Bay of Pigs Invasion of 1961 Cuban Missile Crisis of 1962 highlighted the American government as an incompetent organization that was incapable of managing its own affairs. The public's distrust increased when Lyndon Johnson expanded the war in Vietnam, seeking to win it at any cost. The war became wildly unpopular. It shaped almost every aspect of American life. Songs were made in protest of the war. Professors wrote books condemning violence against a people who had never threatened, nor ever could, threaten America. People appeared on talk shows ready to tell the world what they thought of the war. Demonstrations occurred all across the country.

The nation's people had supported both the government through both World Wars. Even in the midst of great hardship, it was far more likely to find someone who was in favor of the war than someone who was not. Dissent was something new. It had arisen together with broadcast television. Reporters brought images of the war to the homes of every American family. The truth was difficult to conceal- and the truth was that American soldiers brought flamethrowers to small villages where members of the Viet Cong were suspected of living.

Richard Nixon being elected president did nothing to change attitudes everywhere in the country. Martin Luther King and Robert Kennedy were both murdered within months of each other. Those deaths only served to fuel skepticism and outrage within the populace.

As it often happens, skepticism took root in America's universities. The university is a place uniquely suited to the spreading of new ideas. They are often cut off from the rest of the world. They are places where young men and women devote themselves to the process of learning. They learn not only from their professors, but from each other. At any university, an idea is like a germ. It spreads and multiplies through all kinds of people. The type of ideas that spread depend on the people who are there.

On April 30th, 1970, Nixon sent American troops to invade Cambodia. This was only a few months removed from the My Lai Massacre, an event in which hundreds of Vietnamese civilians were killed. College students had also been affected by changes in the draft in 1969. The number of deferments allowed had decreased. Graduate students pursuing their master's degrees were no longer eligible to legally avoid military service. From the perspective of the average American, the war in Vietnam wasn't doing anything other than throwing away the lives of young men and women for no good reason at all. No one saw any reason why Cambodia should be any different.

On Friday, May 1st, a day when students were normally preparing for the weekend, five hundred students began a demonstration. Once it ended, they planned for another one for May 4th. Some students buried the Constitution in an attempt to symbolize how Nixon had done away with it. Things remained peaceful until around midnight.

The riot began as many other riots have begun. People left bars late at night. They threw bottles around, broke car windshields, and shop windows. Even late at night, the news circulated in a short amount of time. Many bars that had been open closed early. This only caused the people in the town to become angrier. The situation went from bad to worse in a short amount of time. Mayor LeRoy Satrom declared a state of emergency. He petitioned the state government for help. However, given the lateness of the hour, it was highly unlikely that help would arrive in a timely manner. People would have to be roused out of their beds.

Police officers used tear gas- a form of chemical weaponry- in an attempt to get the crowd to disperse. This proved unsuccessful. The crowd did not disperse. It merely moved to another part of the town of Kent- towards the campus. Rumors were banded about the town: it was feared that revolutionaries were sent into the town for the purpose of destroying the university.

Mayor Satrom found himself in a quandary. He did not expect that his own police force would be able to quell further disturbances. He requested that the National Guard be sent to the town. Though the request was granted, it took some time before the troops showed up. In the meantime, the campus ROTC building was set on fire. A thousand people cheered. When firefighters and police officers arrived to put the fire out, they were attacked and prevented from doing their duty.

On the morning of Sunday May 3rd, Governor Jim Rhodes went on television. He called the student protesters un-American. He claimed that they were determined to destroy higher education in the state of Ohio. This claim appears to be dubious at best. The protesters were a mix of all kinds of different people. Each of them had their own particular objectives and agendas.

They all shared a single, common trait: they hated the war. They disliked the authority figures that had led the country into war. They hated police officers, elected officials, and anybody else with any amount of authority at all. Rhodes misrepresenting the facts to the public likely did nothing to defray the tensions that had sprang up. Instead, the opposite appears to have occurred.

By 8 PM that night, students that had returned to the college after enjoying their weekend staged a demonstration. The National Guardsmen used tear gas to try and disperse the crowd. A curfew was put into effect. The demonstrators hoped to gain a meeting with Mayor Satrom and the president of the university. Several students were wounded with bayonets. A meeting of any kind appeared unlikely.

A protest was scheduled at noon the following Monday. The university printed out leaflets suggesting that the meeting was canceled. However, more than two thousand people showed up. The National Guard again used tear gas. The wind blew the tear gas away from the crowd. With no way to disperse the crowd, the use of violent force escalated.

At 12:24 PM, the guardsmen fired a total of sixty-seven rounds into the crowd. The guardsmen claimed that a sniper had opened fire upon them. This appears to be an unlikely event, given that many of the university students had no military training themselves. Even presuming that a sniper had been there, firing upon the students would not stop the sniper from firing. It appears likely that guardsmen feared for their lives in the face of unarmed students who didn't want to do anything other than hold speeches and chant slogans.

Four people were killed. Nine others were wounded. The students had dared to protest against a federal government policy they didn't like. History repeated itself once again. Violent force was once again used to stop people who did not approve of what the government had done.

Of course, the students were not entirely without blame. The destruction of private property itself was a crime. Anyone who committed that crime should have been arrested. However, that was not what happened. Students were shot with impunity. Bullets had been used in lieu of negotiation. In a single stroke, the American government had been revealed for what it was: a violent organization that would stop at nothing to have its own way.

This pattern would continue repeating itself every time the citizens of America and the law enforcement agents of the country met each other. Law enforcement officers of the country would continue the job they have always done: suppression of dissent by any means necessary.

Chapter 13: Occupy Wall Street and a Hopeful Conclusion

Income inequality became an increasingly popular topic following the Panic of 2008. Bankers on Wall Street was seen as being irresponsible, even dangerous. Public perception was that they were greedy people who thought nothing of the welfare of others. It was also public knowledge that many corporations sought to buy elections and influence in government. America's problems of increasing poverty, increasing misery, decreasing educational standards, environmental problems could all be blamed on the political process being for sale to the highest bidder.

The movement that would come to be known as Occupy Wall Street was inspired by the Egyptian Revolution of 2011. The events in Egypt had largely been galvanized by people using social media sites such as Facebook. The possibility that people could use social media accounts in order to arrange demonstrations had led to increasingly strict Facebook censorship that continues to the present day. The Occupy movement began in much the same way.

As the bankers who were perceived as being responsible for the panic were not brought to trial, much less arrested, people started to believe that they had to do something on their own. A peaceful occupation of Wall Street was proposed by a Canadian publication called Adbusters in February of 2011.

The initial idea gained steam throughout the year. People of all kinds protested against Wall Street. Though Occupy was socialist in nature, it gained a large following all across America with people who wanted to change society. Movements sprang up in Oakland, San Francisco, Chicago, and elsewhere throughout the nation. Even in small towns such as Harrisburg, Pennsylvania, an Occupy group sprang up. I have a unique perspective on how the group operated. I myself was a part of it.

It was a cold October day when I wandered down Third Street in Harrisburg to the Occupy encampment in front of the state capital. The state government allowed the group to set up shop on the sidewalk. The group was friendly enough; it just wasn't committed to social change. It was far more committed to acquiring free stuff from any place they could get it from. The group attracted its fair of share of homeless people, just as it did in New York.

The police officers in Harrisburg were unlike those that patrolled Wall Street. One night, while I was talking with the other members of Occupy Harrisburg, a drunk man came by. He was there for some time before the police were called in. The police tried to reason with the man. When this proved impossible, the man was hauled away in handcuffs. The police said that we had the right to stay there as long as we wanted. Whether the police officers genuinely felt this way or whether they were simply obeying the instructions they were given remains unclear. It was a happy exception to the rule that governments use force against people who disagree with it.

That rule was played out in America's big cities. In a place called Zuccotti Park in New York, the Occupy encampment had been growing by leaps and bounds. People supplied power to the encampment through bicycling. A small library was developing. People from all walks of life lived in tents. Some took showers. Others did not.

The movement was popular everywhere throughout the nation. Everyone involved recognized that a change had to be made. The Iraq War had been started on a lie that the country possessed weapons of mass destruction, which they did not. The war in Afghanistan continued even after Osama bin Laden was reported dead as of May 2, 2011. Electing a new president had done nothing to change the status quo. Politicians were still corrupt. Bad laws were still being signed. When people voted, they only voted on a handful of the people who actually worked for the government. No one got to vote for the heads of bureaucratic agencies. No one got to vote for Supreme Court judges, or members of the president's cabinet. Much of the government operated outside the approval- oftentimes without informing- of the public. There was no way to provoke a positive change within the government except through protesting.

As people chanted various slogans, police officers arrived with zip ties, handcuffs, and nightsticks. People were arrested by the thousands. They were hauled into the back of police wagons for walking on the sidewalk, or for walking on the street. Many were arrested for resisting arrest. The pretexts upon which people became detained were paper-thin. Some of the arrests came down to nothing more than kidnapping.

Journalists brought video cameras along to the scenes of the demonstrations. They broadcast their videos through a website called UStream. Some of the journalists themselves were arrested. In time, the government began jamming the broadcasts. No one in power wanted people all around the world to see what was actually happening. Despite their best efforts, they largely failed.

It soon became popular to record police officers at any time, and for any reason. The activity was called cop-blocking. A host of websites and social media pages sprang up around cop-blocking. Police officers became to be seen as dangerous. In many departments across the country, candidates were disqualified if they had an IQ above a certain level; only those who were capable of unquestioning obedience would be accepted as new officers. The practice of law enforcement had far more to do with obeying orders than following the law. If the orders an officer receives breaks the law, officers tend to follow their orders rather than object to them.

Few officers objected to treating thousands of protesters like criminals. There were only two sides in the Occupy movement: the side of the government and everyone else. The movement sparked paranoia within government circles. At the end of 2012, the yearly National Defense Authorization Act contained a new proviso that had never before been openly declared in any American legal statue. It was now legal to indefinitely detain a terrorist or any person suspected of aiding a terrorist in any way. Since the definition of a terrorist rested with the government itself, the government had declared that it could arrest and hold anyone for as long as it wanted regardless of what the Constitution had to say particularly the Fifth Amendment.

The Fifth Amendment was written as follows:

No person shall be held to answer for a capital, or otherwise infamous crime, unless on a presentment or indictment of a Grand Jury, except in cases arising in the land or naval forces, or in the Militia, when in actual service in time of War or public danger; nor shall any person be subject for the same offence to be twice put in jeopardy of life or limb; nor shall be compelled in any criminal case to be a witness against himself, nor be deprived of life, liberty, or property, without due process of law; nor shall private property be taken for public use, without just compensation.

Indefinite detention, by its very nature, deprives a person of their liberty without due process of the law. This provision was aimed at making legal mass arrests, if such a possibility would have come to pass. If the entire nation dissented against the government, the government was prepared to arrest the entire nation if necessary. The only way to do so would be to ignore the principles upon which it was founded.

The government appears to have no problem doing so. No state can secede without violent resistance. No protester can agitate for change without meeting violent resistance. The process of voting increasingly appears to be rigged- dead people vote; votes are counted in the way or as negatives; candidates are sued off the ballot; delegates, super delegates, and the Electoral College count more than the popular vote. The system has arranged itself in such a manner as to resist as much change as possible.

Both the people and the politicians of America suffer under this system even while both of them think that the opposite is true. Those who defend the government claim that without it, certain social services would cease to exist. Even if this were true, and there is nothing to suggest that it is or isn't true, the loss of such public services would be a small price to pay in exchange for abolishing institutional violence that is assured by the existence of the government and its proclivity for harming anyone who protests against it or disobeys its edicts. Sending in members of the military to quell dissent is an option that American politicians are all too willing to consider, just as Chinese politicians did during the Tiananmen Square massacre during 1989.

The pattern for every government everywhere in the world remains the same: people are supposed to pay taxes and follow the rules. Elected officials are often exempt from those same rules. As enforcers of the law, creators of the law, and judges of the law, they feel themselves above the law. They act without morality because they believe they decide what the country's morality ought to be.

Negotiating with them only brings temporary gains that are soon reversed. Pro-choice abortion advocates who celebrated the *Roe v. Wade* decision have found that though abortion is legal, it has become inaccessible by means of unusual state regulation sought at denying a woman the right to have an abortion. The victories that human rights advocates achieved during the 1960s have been undone by rampant racism throughout law enforcement agencies of all kinds. Although they have equal rights under the law, they are not treated equally.

The law, especially American law, is a negotiation. It is created subjectively and enforced subjectively. It can change at any moment, and for any reason. Given that individual citizens have little to no say in what laws are proposed or passed, it is clear that each citizen must live under laws that he or she has no stake in making.

The single lesson that the whole of American history teaches is this: the more time passes, the more abrasive and inimical to human life it becomes. This is not a fanciful abstract theory with no basis in fact. The incidents that you have read about up until now all happened. The history of America is a history of men with guns going out to enforce the edicts of men in expensive clothing.

In order to ensure equitable and fair treatment for each person, such a government must be removed or limited as much as possible. History suggests that the less power any government has, the more free people are, the more money those people have, and the more that each citizen is capable of living autonomously. No government program sponsored Harriet Tubman when she wished to free slaves in the American south. No government program sponsored suffragists who wished to gain the right to vote; rather, they were beaten, arrested, and thrown into prison for their trouble. No government program sponsored peace-loving people who gave flowers to police officers as a means of protesting the Vietnam War. No government program sponsored Occupy Wall Street, or any freedom movement which has arisen since then. Each of these programs have arisen independently by people who sincerely wished to change the world for the better. Each and every time, law enforcement officers have been there ready to quash it.

Studying these things has, over the course of many years, convinced me that people naturally want to help others and make their circumstances better. If trust should be placed in anyone, it is in these courageous souls who defy every social norm and standard to do what they think is right. If we can manage it, if we can trust in ourselves rather than in governmental authority, we will all experience the benefits that come from personal liberty.

CPSIA information can be obtained
at www.ICGtesting.com
Printed in the USA
LVHW080128170222
711193LV00013B/855